LCM Exams

Step Examination in Theory of Music

INTRODUCTION

This publication is part of a progressive series of handbooks, primarily intended for candidates considering taking London College of Music graded examinations in Music Theory. However, given each handbook's content of educational material, the series provides a solid foundation of music theory for any music student, of any age, whether they are intending to take an exam or not. Examination candidates *must* use this series in conjunction with the current LCM syllabus.

To enter for an examination, or for further details and syllabuses, please contact:

University of West London
LCM Examinations
St Mary's Road
Ealing
London W5 5RF
tel: 020 8231 2364
e-mail: lcm.exams@uwl.ac.uk
lcme.uwl.ac.uk

or your local representative

D1514137

Keep this book, as you may find it useful when preparing for higher grades.

Published by the University of West London, LCM Publications
St Mary's Road, Ealing, London W5 5RF

ISMN 979 0 57012 034 5
Reprinted 2004
Revised in 2008 and 2010
Reprinted in 2013

By Barry Draycott and Martyn Williams
Music typesetting by Take Note Publishing Ltd.

CONTENTS

Syllabus

1.   Giving the pitch names of notes in either Treble or Bass Clef (candidate's choice). Middle C will be the only leger line note.

2.   Shape and time values of notes and rests from semibreve to quaver.

3.   The following time signatures:

$$\frac{2}{4} \qquad \frac{3}{4} \qquad \frac{4}{4} \ \textbf{(C)}$$

4.   Major scales and key signatures of C, G and F

The Stave and Clefs

Music is written on five lines and in four spaces on the stave (or staff).

In order to show notes of higher and lower pitch we use two staves and two clefs.

For higher notes we use the Treble or G Clef.

For lower notes we use the Bass or F Clef.

Treble Clef – note it 'curls' around the 2nd line.

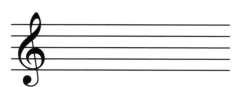

Bass Clef – note it 'curls' around the 4th line.

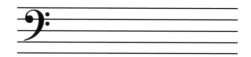

This is known as the Treble Stave.

This is known as the Bass Stave.

Exercises

Practise writing the Treble Clef.

Start here – remember it begins by 'curling' around the 2nd line.

Practise writing the Bass Clef.

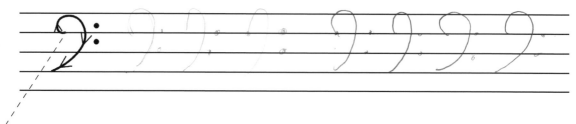

Start here – remember it begins by 'curling' around from the 4th line. Don't forget the two dots as shown – one above and one below the 4th line.

Notation

Notes are given letter names.

The musical alphabet is only 7 letters:

A B C D E F G -

and then repeats in order.

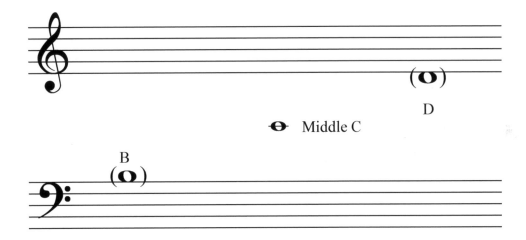

Middle C is so named because it is written on its own short line between the Treble Stave and Bass Stave.

On the Treble Stave the note above Middle C will be D and on the Bass Stave the note below Middle C will be B.

Think of the musical alphabet: A   │ B C D │   E F G

Here are all the notes on the Treble Stave.

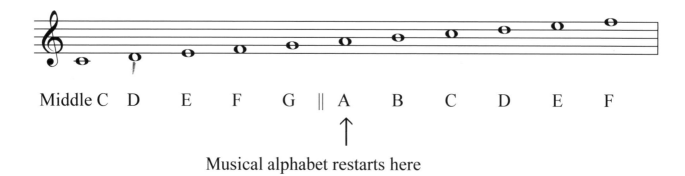

Middle C D   E   F   G ‖ A   B   C   D   E   F

↑

Musical alphabet restarts here

Here are all the notes on the Bass Stave.

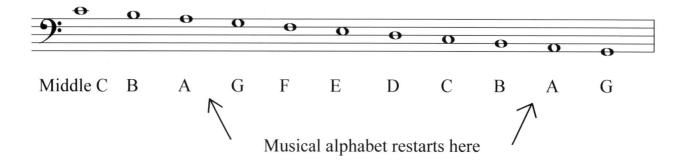

Middle C B   A   G   F   E   D   C   B   A   G

Musical alphabet restarts here

Note. 1) When the notes move *up* the stave the musical alphabet goes forward
(i.e. the notes get *higher* in sound).

2) When the notes move *down* the stave the musical alphabet goes backwards
(i.e. the notes get *lower* in sound).

Exercises

Write the following notes using the Treble Clef.

↑
A   D   F   G   B   Middle C   E

Put in
Treble Clef

Write the following notes using the Bass Clef.

↑
G   F   B   D   Middle C   A   E

Put in
Bass Clef

Give the letter names of these notes.

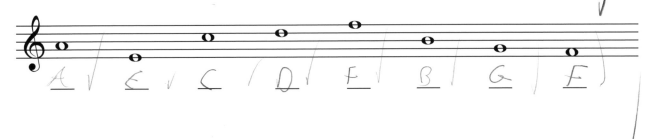

A   E   C   D   F   B   G   E

Give the letter names of these notes.

G   C   E   G   B   A   A   D

Note Values

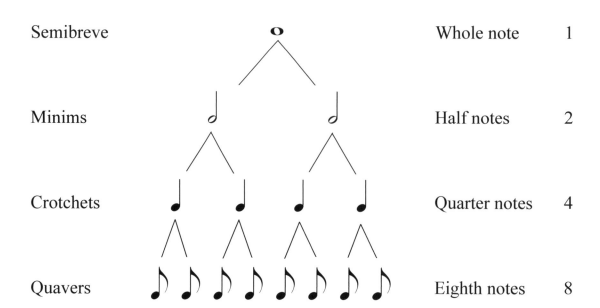

Semibreve	𝅝	Whole note	1
Minims		Half notes	2
Crotchets		Quarter notes	4
Quavers		Eighth notes	8

Looking at the above table we can see:

𝅝 = 2 minims or 4 crotchets or 8 quavers.

𝅗𝅥 = 2 crotchets or 4 quavers.

𝅘𝅥 = 2 quavers.

OR

𝅝 = 𝅗𝅥 𝅗𝅥 or 𝅘𝅥 𝅘𝅥 𝅘𝅥 𝅘𝅥 or 𝅘𝅥𝅮 𝅘𝅥𝅮 𝅘𝅥𝅮 𝅘𝅥𝅮 𝅘𝅥𝅮 𝅘𝅥𝅮 𝅘𝅥𝅮 𝅘𝅥𝅮

𝅗𝅥 = 𝅘𝅥 𝅘𝅥 or 𝅘𝅥𝅮 𝅘𝅥𝅮 𝅘𝅥𝅮 𝅘𝅥𝅮

𝅘𝅥 = 𝅘𝅥𝅮 𝅘𝅥𝅮

Exercises

Refer to the chart on page 8.

Write the name and value below these notes.

_____

Write the following as one note:

♩ + ♩ =   𝅗𝅥 + ♩ + ♩ =

♪ + ♪ =   ♩ + ♩ + ♩ + ♪ + ♪ =

♩ + ♪ + ♪ =   𝅗𝅥 + ♪ + ♪ + ♩ =

Write the following as two notes:

♩ =

𝅝 =

𝅗𝅥 =

Fill in the * missing note to make the correct value:

♩ + *   = 𝅗𝅥   ♪ + ♩ + *   = 𝅗𝅥

♪ + *   = ♩   ♩ + ♩ + *   = 𝅝

𝅗𝅥 + ♩ + *   = 𝅝   ♪ + ♪ + *   = 𝅗𝅥

9

Exercises

Refer to the chart on page 8.

How many different ways can you write groups of notes which equal these single notes:

1)   𝅝   Write 3 different groups

2)   𝅗𝅥   Write 2 different groups

3)   𝅘𝅥   Write 1 group

Grouping Notes

This only applies to quavers at this level.

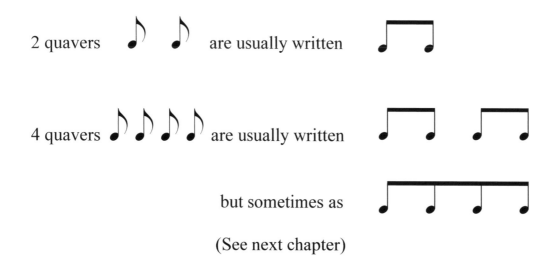

2 quavers   𝅘𝅥𝅮   𝅘𝅥𝅮   are usually written

4 quavers 𝅘𝅥𝅮 𝅘𝅥𝅮 𝅘𝅥𝅮 𝅘𝅥𝅮 are usually written

but sometimes as

(See next chapter)

Time

Music is measured in bars – using barlines *

Each bar has the same number of beats.

The beats in each bar are equal.

The above has 3 ♩ beats to each bar.

However you may for each or some of the beats use notes which add up to a crotchet.

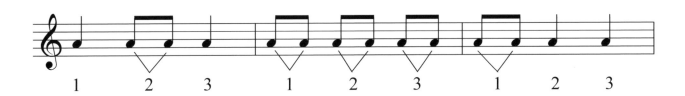

You may also use notes which add the beats together.

In order to make things clear – we write a 'time signature' at the beginning of the first line of the piece.

The *top figure* tells you the number of beats in each bar.

The *lower figure* tells you the value of each beat.

So the examples on page 11 would have the following time signature:

3 ← 3 beats per bar.

4 ← value of each beat is a crotchet (or ¼ note – see chart on page 8).

The time signature is placed after the clef.

OR

The time signatures for this level are:

1)   **2/4**   2)   **3/4**   3)   **4/4 (C)**

1) has 2 ♩ beats per bar.

2) has 3 ♩ beats per bar.

3) has 4 ♩ beats per bar.

Here are some examples. Bar 1 of each shows the simple number of beats and their value; bar 2 shows groups of notes forming 1 beat; and bar 3 shows notes adding the beats together.

1)

2)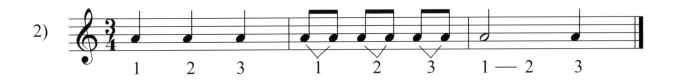

3)

In example 3 you will see 4 ♪'s all joined together. This happens in **4/4** if the ♪'s are beats 1 and 2 or beats 3 and 4.

13

Exercises

Put in the time signature at * for each of these bars:

Write 3 bars of notes in the following times.

Add notes at * to make the correct number of beats in each bar.

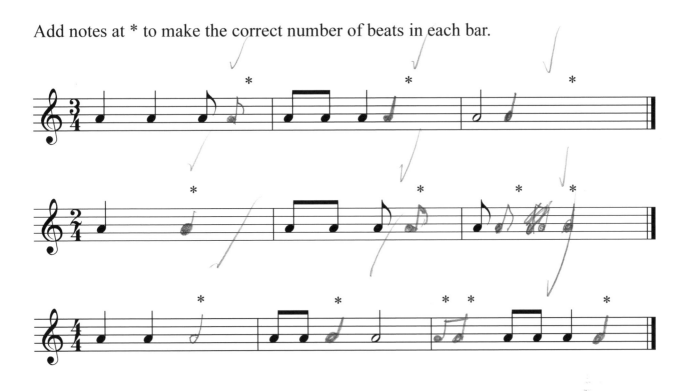

Sometimes you will be asked to correct bars which have too many notes, and therefore are incorrect in relation to the time signature.

Cross out the notes not required.

Exercises

In each bar cross out 1 note to make the correct number of beats.

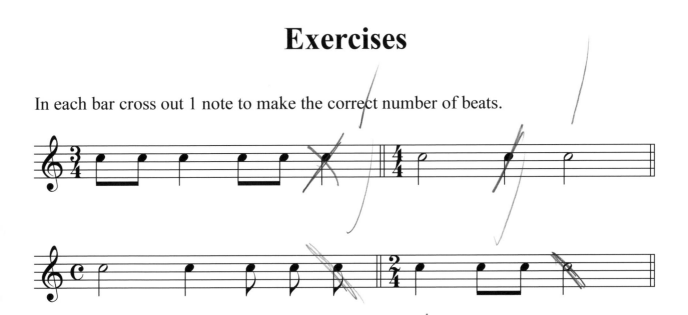

Rests

Notes produce a sound – rests produce silence. This gives a variety in music, and rests are sometimes called 'the golden sound of music'. They can often be dramatic!

Each note value has an equivalent rest value.

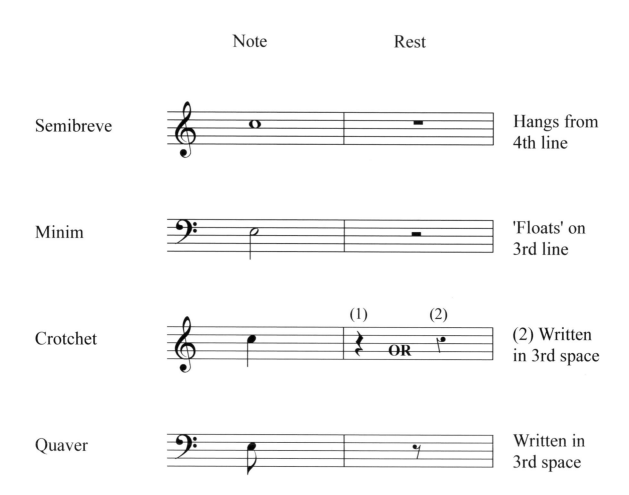

	Note	Rest	
Semibreve			Hangs from 4th line
Minim			'Floats' on 3rd line
Crotchet		(1) OR (2)	(2) Written in 3rd space
Quaver			Written in 3rd space

Rests replace the value of the note. The beats of the bar are clearly shown.

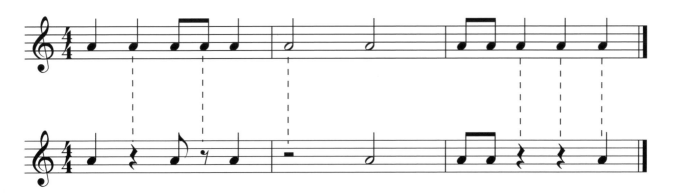

Exercises

Rewrite the following replacing the notes at * with a rest.

Add rests at * to complete the correct number of beats in each bar. Remember to show the crotchet beats.

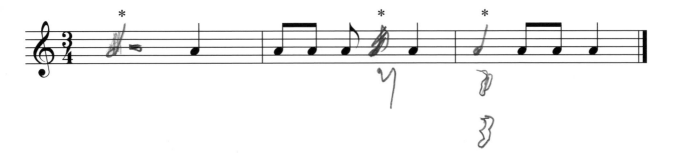

Scales

The scales you will need to know are:

C major

G major

F major

All scales have 8 notes (an octave) – they begin on the letter name of the scale and end on the same letter name an octave higher.

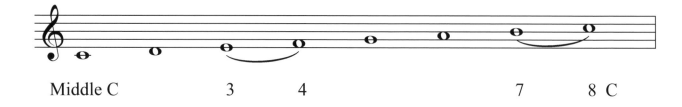

Middle C   3   4   7   8 C

This is the scale of C major – the Ancient Greeks used this scale but they called it the 'Ionian Mode'. Notice notes 3 & 4 and 7 & 8 are slurred in the above example to show the position of *semitones* (half steps).

Look at the piano / keyboard.

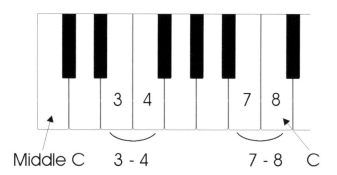

You will see that no notes occur between notes 3 & 4 and 7 & 8, i.e. between E & F and B & C on the piano. Because of this these are called semitones.

In each Major Scale the semitones always occur between notes 3-4 and 7-8. If this does not happen we have to alter one note to get the right sound.

To do this we can use a 'sharp' or 'flat'.
         a sharp (♯) raises a note by a semitone.
         a flat (♭) lowers a note by a semitone.

Here are the notes for the scale of G major.

Play this on the keyboard – something sounds 'wrong' with the note *.

If we put a sharp before this note (and play the black note above) it will now sound correct.

Now the semitones occur where we need them – between notes 3 & 4 and 7 & 8.

Here are the notes for the scale of F major.

Play them on the keyboard.

You will find that the 4th note (*) will sound wrong. If we lower this note a semitone by placing a flat (♭) before it and play the black note below – the scale will sound correct.

Play this on the keyboard.

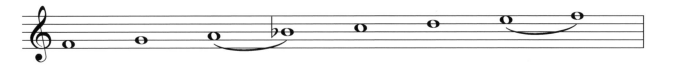

Again the semitones occur between notes 3 & 4 and 7 & 8.

Writing the scales of G and F with 'accidentals' [1] before the notes which need them is one way of writing these scales.

The other way is to use a key signature – that is the sharp or flat needed is written at the beginning of the music, *between* the clef and time signature.

G major ascending – going up. (With key signature of F♯.)

In G major, the F♯ key signature means that every F will be played as F♯.

G major descending – going down.

F major ascending. (With key signature of B♭.)

F major descending.

[1] *Accidentals* are sharps and flats. Naturals (♮) are also accidentals, and are explained at a later stage.

Exercises

Write the following key signatures:

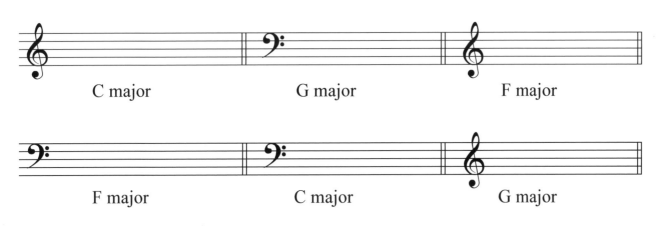

C major   G major   F major

F major   C major   G major

Write the following scales in either Treble or Bass clefs.

1)   F major with key signature, ascending (upwards).

2)   G major without key signature, descending (downwards). (Use accidentals.)

3)   F major without key signature, ascending. (Use accidentals.)

4)   C major, descending.

5)   G major with key signature, ascending.

N.B. C major needs no key signature or accidentals.

Remember the notes needing accidentals are found by counting from the lowest note!

Put in the necessary accidentals to make the following scales.

F major

G major

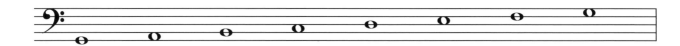

G major

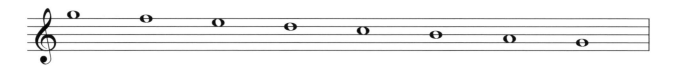

F major

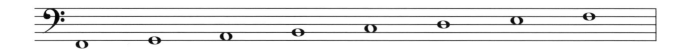

Sometimes you will be given a few bars of music and asked to add *either* a key signature *or* accidentals to put the music into a key.

e.g.   Add accidentals to make this tune in F major.

Add accidentals to make this tune in G major.

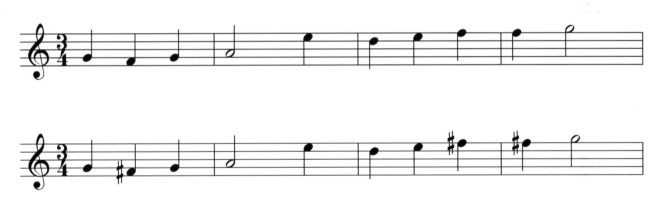

Remember that an accidental lasts for a whole bar.

OR   Name the keys of the following.

Key: _____

Key: _____

General Hints

1. Use a sharp pencil, an HB is best.

2. Write neatly.

3. Notes must be clearly written on lines or in spaces.

4. Write rests carefully as shown on page 16.

5. Place ♯s or ♭s carefully.

6. Remember that above the 3rd line stems of notes usually turn *down*.

Specimen Paper A

(10)

1. **Either** (a) Give the letter names of these notes.

Name _____

OR (b) Give the letter names of these notes.

Name _____

2. [a] Give the *time values* of these notes in part or whole crotchets, then after each note write   (10)
   a rest of the same value at *.

Value _____

   [b] Write one note which is twice the value of the given note.

3. Give the *total* value of these bars in crotchet beats.

(10)

Value _____   _____

4. Write the following note groups as *one* note.   (10)

i)   ii)   iii)   iv)   v)

5. **Either** Write the major scale starting on this note. Add the correct key signature. (10)

OR

(Downwards)

(Upwards)

6. Name the keys of these two melodies. (10)

EITHER (a)

Key _____

Key _____

OR (b)

Key _____

Key _____

7. At the * put in the correct time signature. (10)

8. Add a note at the * to make the correct number of beats for the time signature shown. (10)

9. In each bar cross out ONE NOTE to make the correct number of beats for the time signature shown. (20)

Specimen Paper B

1. **Either** (a) Give the letter names of these notes. (10)

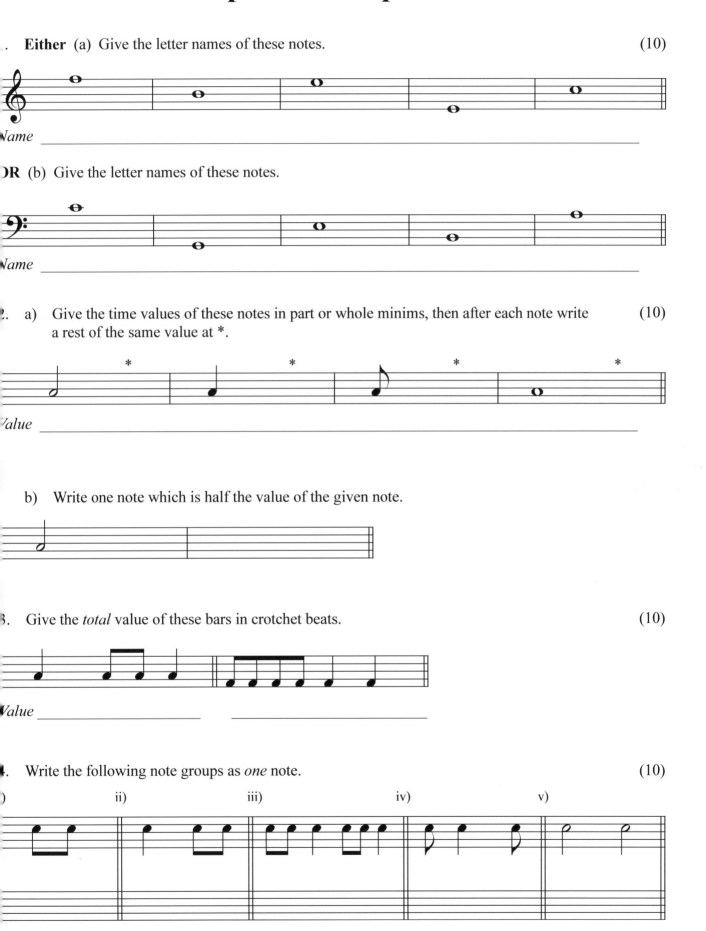

Name _____

OR (b) Give the letter names of these notes.

Name _____

2. a) Give the time values of these notes in part or whole minims, then after each note write a rest of the same value at *. (10)

Value _____

b) Write one note which is half the value of the given note.

3. Give the *total* value of these bars in crotchet beats. (10)

Value _____

4. Write the following note groups as *one* note. (10)

                ii)   iii)   iv)   v)

5. a) Write the scale of C major ascending (going up) from the given note.　(10)

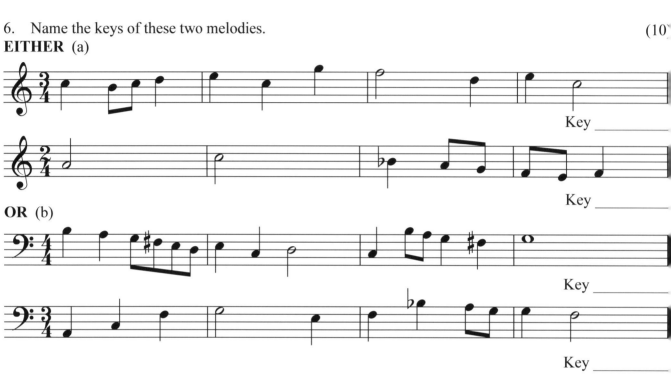

b) Write the scale of G major descending (going down) from the given note. Add the
   correct key signature.

6. Name the keys of these two melodies.　(10)
EITHER (a)

Key _____

Key _____

OR (b)

Key _____

Key _____

7. At the * put in the correct time signature.　(10)

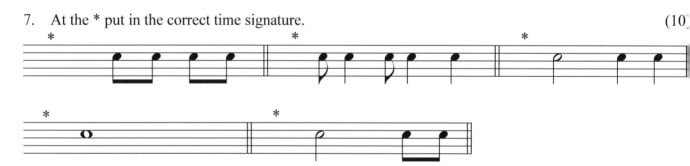

8. Add a rest at each * to make the correct number of beats in each bar for the time signature shown. (10)

9. In each bar cross out ONE NOTE to make the correct number of beats for the time　(20)
    signature shown.